Encouraging Words

By: Leta Jones

Copyright © 2015 by Leta Jones

All rights reserved. No part of this publication may be reproduced, stored in a retrieval system or transmitted in any form or by any means – electronic, mechanical, photocopying, and recording or otherwise – without the prior written permission of the author, except for brief passages quoted by a reviewer in a newspaper or magazine. To perform any of the above is an infringement of copyright law.

Scripture taken from the HOLY BIBLE, NEW INTERNATIONAL VERSION®. NIV®. Copyright © 1973, 1978, 1984 by International Bible Society. Used by permission of Zondervan. All rights reserved worldwide.

Scripture quotations marked (TLB) are taken from The Living Bible copyright © 1971. Used by permission of Tyndale House Publishers, Inc., Carol Stream, Illinois 60188. All rights reserved.

Library and Archives Canada Cataloguing in Publication
Jones, Leta, 1932 -

ISBN: 13: 978-1517224868
ISBN-10: 1517224861

Cover art by Cindy Ryon
Cover design by Matt Morrison
Photography by Geoff Howard

To order or request information, please email:
aspecialplace@telus.net

Foreword

I must admit that seeing the words "Leta Jones" on the cover of a book took a little getting used to. To me, this book was not written by "Leta Jones," it was written by "Pomma." Family lore tells the story that when I was just learning to talk; I could not pronounce "Grandma" properly. Instead, "Pomma" is what came out of my young mouth. As a family, we have been using that word ever since. While the Pomma story is no legend, the real Pomma, Leta Jones is certainly a legend for the ages. People sometime ask me what the difference is between a Pomma and a Grandma. On a family tree there may be little difference. They are the same title. In person, however, a grandma is a lot different than a Pomma. I often tell people, "Grandmas make cookies but Pommas make history." Leta Jones, my grandma, is one of the most genuine people I know. She loves well and is loved by everyone. Her family adores her. Her friends are fiercely loyal to her. She is loved at her church, in her community and now she is even loved as an author.

Her first book, "There's No Rehearsal...This Is It!" was a collection of timeless truths gleaned from her life-long reflections.

They were stories from a life that has been well lived. A life not without a great deal of pain, heartbreak, confusion and trial. But life that was dedicated, principled and full of zeal towards the things that matter most. I benefited from that first book immensely. It was not only full of moments that forged my family's history, it was also the story of a faithful God revealing himself to and through one of His most amazing saints. Since that first book was so well received, another one had to follow it up. That is the book of encouragement you now hold in your hands today.

I am thankful that the stories in this present volume are ones that I have heard many times on our walks together, over Pomma's famous home-made waffles and in the many letters that she has sent me over the years. These stories have shaped me to be the man, the pastor, the husband and father that I am today; the man that my "praying grandma" has also believed that I could be.

It is now my pleasure to have a small part in introducing these stories to you. May they point you to the one thing that Pomma would desire the most — to Jesus Christ and the lavish love that He has for all of us.

As you read this book, listen to the story that He is telling you through Leta. This book is a collection of stories about one of the most amazing parts of God's grace: that God uses ordinary people to make an extraordinary impact on others. That is what Leta has sought to do here. I hope you enjoy it, that it touches your heart, encourages you on your journey, helps you encourage others on theirs and that it brings you closer to God.

By: Jon Morrison
Pastor and Author of Clear Minds & Dirty Feet

Acknowledgments

I want to thank a few special people without whom; this book would never have been written.

Cindy Ryon, artist, friend, walking partner and encourager. You are one of God's gems and I will always appreciate your excellent work in everything you tackle. Thank you especially for keeping me on track when everything went sideways. You not only gave me your first oil painting, but wanted me to have it for the cover of this book.

My two daughters, Wendy Brown and Patti Morrison. I thank you for the many suggestions, corrections and above all you saw the struggles and gave me hope to finish. Patti, you have always been in whatever corner I've found myself and helped me get out. Wendy and Patti, I trust your comments and all the help you offer unconditionally for me.

Geoff Howard, my nephew and photographer. Thank you Geoff for jumping in whenever I call you and making it such a fun experience getting pictures taken.

Jon Morrison, my eldest grandson and an accomplished author of three books. Thank you for your helpful words and encouragement.

Matt Morrison, my grandson, co-founder of Church OS, where he shares his talent to create amazing web designs for churches and small businesses. Thank you for sharing your expertise in creating the cover designs to complete this book.

Table of Contents

Introduction 1

Chapter 1 .... **3**

Everyone Needs Encouraging Words 2

    You Never Know 3

Chapter 2 .... **3**

Heavenly Nudges 6

    Window of Opportunity – Writer's Course 7

    African Widow 9

    He Knew My Next Address 13

    Moment Makers 16

    Song of Praise 17

Chapter 3 .... **19**

Words Make A Difference 18

    One Word 18

    Two Words 21

    Three Words 25

    Four Words 27

    Five Words 30

Chapter 4 33

Happiness Is 32

Acts of Kindness 33

Friendships 35

A New Friend 36

Words To A Friend...38

Using Your Gifts 40

Talker and Listener 42

Art's 25th Anniversary Surprise....................44

Mom's 80th Birthday Surprise.......................45

Surprise Kidnapped Weekend........................48

Chapter 5 51

Interruptions Can Look Like This 50

Interruptions 51

Alone – But Not Lonely..................................52

Chapter 6 57

Hints for Contentment 56

These Are A Few of My Favourite Things 58

More of My Favourite Things 60

Unexpected Phone Call 62

What Gives Me Joy 63

Time 65

Time, A Precious Gift 66

Chapter 7 69

Every Day Count Your Blessings 68

Gift of Morning 69

Live In The Moment 70

White Spaces 72

The Choices We Make 75

Encouraging Others 76

Voicemail 77

Special Reminders 78

Chapter 8 81

Memory Moments 80

Under Construction 81

God's Blueprint For Your Life 86

Unexpected Gestures 87

The Cross In My Pocket 89

Encouraging Books 90

Uplifting Scriptures 92

My Child ... God Really Loves You 92

Final Thoughts 97

Introduction

For years I've had this book in my head. It has been a journey writing about my experiences, strength and hope. Many encouragers saw a need and put into action what they could do for someone else.

People shared with me their struggles as well as how they finally got through their tough times. The following pages give you words to help others in both their good and difficult times.

A simple note can be held and read over and over again. Words are powerful communication when people are hurting. Stories of how different people were surprised may inspire you to do the same.

Be uplifted knowing God is always there for you and cares deeply no matter what is happening in your life.

I have included Bible verses throughout this book as each one has brought me encouragement at different stages in my life. May they be a blessing and joy to you as well.

Everyone Needs Encouraging Words

"Kind words can be short and easy to speak but their echoes are truly endless." Mother Teresa

Regardless of our age, young or old we welcome words to uplift us. Perhaps you have experienced a few of the situations I've listed.

℘ In our busy lives today we may forget many are hurting.

℘ Different situations require different encouraging words.

℘ Unexpected changes in our lives can cause upsets.

℘ The loss of a family member or friend is traumatic.

℘ Young children respond to encouragement.

℘ A kind word to teenagers may change their actions.

℘ Husbands and wives need to encourage each other.

℘ Grandparents often feel forgotten.

℘ Retired men and women face new challenges.

When we lose our way with losses or changes in our life styles, encouraging words may be exactly what we need to keep going. Everyone experiences up and down times. Words in person, by a telephone call or note might be exactly the right time to give others the motivation to begin again.

Chapter 1

"An anxious heart weighs a man down but a kind word cheers him up." Proverbs 12:25

You Never Know

Many years ago on a trip to Hawaii my husband and I met a very special man called Jack Howard. Over coffee after attending a meeting he shared his life story with us. Jack was in his senior years. I remember listening and enjoying his enthusiastic joy.

At the end of our time with him he reached into his wallet and gave us a poem he wrote and signed his signature at the bottom.

You Never Know

You never know when a word
In something you might say
Will open up for someone
The door that swung one way
You never know when someone
Whose had a real bad nite
Would like to learn the way you live
But you never know – they might

And just in case they didn"t hear
That the door will swing both ways
Their future would be guaranteed
With may happy days
And so it seems it's worth a try
A try with all our might
Of course it may not matter at all
But then again – it might

Jack Howard

Heavenly Nudges

Over the years I've responded in the following ways:

꿍 BE PATIENT, the nudge may not make sense at first.

꿍 Don't resist.

꿍 Pray and ask for help.

꿍 Get a journal.

꿍 Start writing and date it.

William Wordsworth said, *"To begin,"* he wrote, *"begin."*

꿍 Trust and follow through.

꿍 God's timing is likely not yours.

꿍 Ask for confirmation, scripture or a word from someone.

꿍 Share this with a friend or mentor.

꿍 God understands.

꿍 There is nothing too difficult for Him.

꿍 He remembers even if we forget.

꿍 Thank Him and ask for His help.

Chapter 2

"Commit to the Lord whatever you do, and your plans will succeed." Proverbs 16:3

A heavenly nudge is that little voice in my head that prompts me to do something, wait, or asks me a question. I know it has been God guiding and directing me. I've shared a few of these stories in the following pages.

Walt Disney said, *"The way to get things started is to stop talking and start doing."*

Window of Opportunity – Writer's Course

"I will instruct you and teach you in the way you should go."
Psalm 32:8

In early December of 2005 I was in the middle of dealing with details after the recent death of my father. As I picked up the envelopes in my mailbox I noticed one from the Long Ridge Writers' Group in Connecticut regarding a writing course.

On my "someday" list was to write my personal history in story form for my family. This was definitely not the right time. Curious, I opened the material and found a little pamphlet with a couple of short exercises to complete plus instructions to write a short story of two hundred and fifty words before returning it to the sender. They would evaluate my writing and see if I was an acceptable candidate. I took time to complete the exercises but made a huge mess and decided to not send it. Several days later, I received a second pamphlet encouraging me to reply.

I felt this was a "window of opportunity" confirming that God does not work the way we often do and never gives up on us. The one item that caught my eye was, *"If we accept you, you will be assigned a personal mentor."* Immediately, I recognized a mentor was the missing piece I needed. I submitted my writing and was accepted with wonderful comments on my short story.

The two year course with twelve assignments challenged me. I purchased a computer, which stretched my understanding of technology.

This learning curve increased my desire to finally complete the family history. Several of the stories in my first book called "There's No Rehearsal ... This Is It" were lessons from this course. My mentor Tom Hyman's expertise and suggestions carried me through some tough struggles and long nights.

I've been reminded many times that God's timing is definitely not mine. He doesn't make mistakes. It's always a surprise when I follow His nudges but I never regret that plan of action.

African Widow

A new friend and I were walking along the beautiful seawall in West Vancouver. Ann and I had just met through her daughter. I asked about her many trips to Kenya. On my list of "someday" was a mission trip.

"Why don't you come?" she asked.

I told her the timing was wrong for me now. She began to share her stories from Africa and I put it on my heart to go sometime but soon forgot about it.

One morning the following year as I was doing my morning time praying and reading. I vividly remember hearing that small voice saying, *"It's time to call Ann."* My pulse accelerated. I knew it was time to contact Ann. I didn't call but sent her a note and at the end I remember writing, *"Are you going to Africa this year?"*

Ann called from her home in Denver and said, *"We're going in a couple of weeks. Can you join us?"*

It was a wonderful experience with many stories I'll never forget.

We were involved with several projects. One was to begin building a home for a widow. She had nothing but a small shack with two tiny rooms for herself, her son, daughter and also a niece.

Smiling she welcomed us. Ann asked if we could see her home. Just inside three sacks of food staples leaned against the wall on a dirt floor. At the end of the tiny entrance was a single shelf holding supplies and containers. The wall behind was filled with cardboard clippings. She had so little.

I could feel my heart pounding as this gentle, gracious woman showed hospitality like I'd never witnessed. We peeked around the corner into the tiny second room with wall to wall bunks, clothes hanging across the ceiling and I knew I was going to cry. Quickly I said to Ann, *"I have to go back to the van"* and rushed out not wanting the widow to see my tears. I just made it to the bus when I began weeping.

This simple, African lady had nothing, but could open her home to a family member who needed to go to school. This lady did something about it. She was so grateful for everything and her smile and warmth put me to shame.

Our team saw this widow many times around the area to be cleared. She was always the same. I know I will remember her example. What a legacy her children have inherited from their Mom.

At home we need to have an attitude adjustment, count our blessings and pass help on to those that need it.

On another day, at the house of the widow, we saw men with rough and callous hands banging rocks all day in the sweltering heat.

They needed to add them to the cement to be poured. I asked what they would receive for all their hard work. It was $2.50 a day!

Africa continues to remind me to get involved whenever God nudges, prods or brings to my attention those who need help. This trip opened my eyes in ways I'd never experienced.

He Knew My Next Address

June of 2012, Brenda, a friend of mine, was walking near my apartment and saw me reading a large development sign stipulating that the owner of my building was planning to tear it down. At that time I distinctly heard, *"Get ready."*

Brenda asked, *"Leta, what are you going to do?"*

I told her I'd have to move.

She asked where?

I replied, *"God already knows my next address, He just hasn't told me yet."*

It's now six months later, New Year's Eve December 31, 2012 at 5:15 p.m. I'm waiting for my friend Bev who is coming to have dinner and stay the night. My phone rings and I hear a bubbly voice speaking quickly and excited about her new job. I hadn't heard from her for many months as I tried to recall her name. Silently, I'm praying *"Lord, tell me who this is as I know we've been friends for a long time."*

She's asking me if I know of anyone looking for a part-time job and wants to give me the number of the hiring manager. Trying to buy time and praying for her name to come to mind I said, *"Just a moment, I need to get a pen!"*

I took down all the information while still praying when I heard myself ask, *"What was your last job?"*

"Cobbs," she says.

"Oh yes Brenda, I remember!"

After updating our lives and just before we said goodbye Brenda asked, *"Oh, do you know of anyone who would love to have a wonderful apartment and could move by Feb. 1?"*

"Me!" I yelled into the phone.

Brenda said, *"I thought you'd moved. Hang up! I'm going to call the owner and tell him if he hasn't rented yet to give you the apartment."*

Since hearing from that small voice six months ago, *"Get ready!"* I'd been scaling down expecting to move.

Every time I looked in the paper for a suite I would hear, *"Don't you trust me?"* I would put the paper away. I knew God would find a place for me.

I hung up the phone and was in shock. Would the owner be home New Year's Eve?

A few minutes passed and the phone rang. It was the owner who asked if I could meet him in twenty minutes at the apartment which was seven blocks away.

We met, I signed the lease and moved the next month.

Sometimes when prayers aren't answered immediately, I've experienced that God knows best and in His time all things work together for good if you believe.

In my prayers I had asked for five things: affordable, same neighbourhood, less stairs, sunny apartment to see nature and close to transportation. God gave me everything I prayed for plus many more blessings.

"...for your Father knows what you need before you ask Him." Matthew 6:8

Moment Makers

God gets our attention in many ways. His voice comes through as only He can. The following story happened on March 22, 2004 during my quiet time in the morning. I will never forget that day.

I was reading my bible and other devotional books. Suddenly, I heard, *"Pick up your pen!"*

That's strange I thought and continued to read.

A second time only a little louder was, *"Pick up your pen!"* I had never experienced anything like this before and kept on reading.

The third time, very loud in my ears, I heard, *"PICK UP YOUR PEN!"*

Quickly, I obeyed and with my pen flying across the page, I wrote the following song. In the background the music of Blessed Assurance was softly playing.

I had never written a single verse, poem or song before.

My pen didn't stop until the last word "impart" was on the page.

Song of Praise

I have a story, I have a song
To be a blessing helping others be strong.
Each day is my challenge, be it happy or down
Praising my Saviour who walks me along.
He is the answer to questions I have,
Because of my struggles, He knows them so well
So today I will come to His peace for a rest
And ask for more patience and take a deep breath.
Thank you dear Jesus for the price that you paid
Knowing I'd fail you again and again.
Today is a fresh start as I take up my part
I pray just to follow and Your love impart.

By: Leta Jones © March 22, 2004
Original Artwork by Cindy Ryon © 2005

Words Make A Difference

One Word

To Encourage Others:

      ℑ Cherish

      ℑ Value

ℑ Please   ℑ Adore

ℑ Treasure   ℑ Protect

ℑ Approachable   ℑ Appreciate

ℑ Spontaneous   ℑ Love

ℑ Intentional   ℑ Trust

ℑ Understanding   ℑ Patience

ℑ Believe   ℑ Confidential

ℑ Time   ℑ Care

ℑ Meet   ℑ Pray

ℑ Remember   ℑ Protect

"Friendship is the most precious privilege that this earthly experience can offer." Joyce Grenfell, Friendship, 2008

Chapter 3

"A word aptly spoken is like apples of gold in settings of silver."
Proverbs 25:11

What Does It Mean To Be Cherished?

I was married for forty-one years to George Jones. As in every marriage we had our difficulties and challenges. We met when I was fourteen and he was eighteen. From the beginning, he opened doors for me, pulled my chair away from the table for me and showed in many ways his love for me. I always felt protected and special because of his actions.

George was always interested in whatever I was doing and wanted to be a part of it. Over the years we planned and participated in many events.

One memory was his job on a committee to order, unpack and check for breakage of 500 multi-coloured candleholders. We worked well together and he often said, "I couldn't have done it without you," or a simple, *"thanks honey."*

Storms, family issues, losses and unexpected troubles came into our lives. In addition, the hidden giant called alcoholism was creeping ever faster on us. We survived and worked through recovery together knowing God would guide us. George found sobriety in A.A. and stayed sober until his death twenty three years later.

I treasure the word "cherish" as a blessing. I not only felt it by my husband's actions, but also by his words.

Two Words

To Encourage Others:

℘ Thank you

℘ Just begin

℘ Have dreams

℘ Be happy

℘ Be friendly

℘ You're special – note to a friend   ℘ I'm sorry

℘ You're precious – new parents   ℘ Tell me

℘ I remember - reconnecting   ℘ Why not

℘ Bless you – to a friend   ℘ Call someone

℘ I believe - encouraging   ℘ Yes please

℘ Well done – service to you   ℘ Show me

℘ Call again – new friend   ℘ Pray

℘ Good job – kids around the house   ℘ Protect

DON'T ARGUE and DON'T ARGUE. These words have been such a comfort to me when friends or relatives have fallen into memory loss, dementia and worse. I asked a friend who had experienced this problem with a family member. Dale said, *"Don't argue and don't argue."*

Thank You

A courteous word for service performed is often forgotten. I read an inspiring true story from author and international speaker Zig Ziglar.

He and a group of six friends had booked a quiet spot in a restaurant for their dinner meeting. Their dishes and glasses were refilled and cleared away. Coffee was served as their meeting progressed. Their waiter moved quietly and professionally without interrupting them.

After the meal, all six men and Zig Ziglar wrote a short note, along with a 25% tip, thanking the waiter for his service that made their time together memorable and productive.

Talking outside before the men broke up they heard a loud voice calling, *"Wait, please wait."*

Turning around the men saw their waiter dashing towards them with tears on his face. He told them in 25 years, working as a waiter this was the most special and unforgettable thing that had ever happened. No one had ever taken the time to write and thank him for his service. He said, *"Thank you"* and returned to work.

Is there someone you could thank for their service?

There's something about a written note that is special.

Different Ways To Say Thank You

A florist friend of mine shared this touching story. A young man made a decision many years ago to do something special for his Mom once a year. I heard about this when he was celebrating his fortieth birthday.

He came into the florist shop to place an order for a "special lady." Forty beautiful roses were to be delivered in a long florist box with a personal card tucked inside. The card read, *"My life has been special because of you. Thanks Mom for having me!"*

It Doesn't Take Much ... But It Does Take Something!

A woman who worked for a large company in the 1960's told me this story. Her boss was always very appreciative of her work and frequently acknowledged her by words or a note.

Every Secretaries Day there was something special on her desk. She worked early hours and on this day, no matter what time she arrived, there was a beautiful single rose in a lovely container with a note that read, *"I appreciate you."*

Three Words

To Encourage Others:

WRITE A NOTE

℘ Thanks for sharing

℘ Who taught you

FAMILY WORDS

℘ You're my hero

℘ I love you

℘ Thanks for asking

℘ Want a ride

℘ Just for today

℘ I treasure you

℘ Our friendship's special

℘ How's your day

℘ Come with me

℘ Can you talk

Elsie, a wonderful mentor of mine, had the following words prominently displayed on her kitchen bulletin board. This was such an encouragement to me each time I visited her.

GOD SAID IT

I BELIEVE IT

THAT SETTLES IT

Don't Forget

Consider giving words of encouragement to the following people in your life.

PROFESSIONAL PEOPLE:

- ℑ Teachers
- ℑ Professors
- ℑ Politicians
- ℑ Journalists
- ℑ Editors
- ℑ Doctors
- ℑ Nurses
- ℑ Care Workers
- ℑ Writers

Without words or appreciation shown by people, many will fail and never recover.

- ℑ Retirees
- ℑ Baby sitters
- ℑ Apartment managers
- ℑ Paper boys or girls
- ℑ Car mechanics
- ℑ Neighbours

Four Words

The following words and questions help us communicate with others as we share our experiences, strength and hope. May they be useful to you.

QUESTIONS TO ASK YOUR MENTOR:

ℑ How did you change?

ℑ What did you do?

ℑ What was the hardest?

ℑ Who was your model?

ℑ Were you ever insecure?

ℑ How did you survive?

ℑ What makes you happy?

TALKING WITH A FRIEND:

ℑ Thank you for listening

ℑ You made me smile

ℑ Tell me your secret

ℑ I love your enthusiasm

ℑ What makes you happy?

"I keep the telephone of my mind open to peace, harmony, health, love and abundance. Whenever doubt, anxiety, or fear try to call me, they will get a busy signal and soon they will forget my number." Edith Armstrong, 2008 Friendship Book

Blessings of Mentors

"Listen to advice and accept instruction, and in the end you will be wise." Proverbs 19:20

I've had two wonderful mentors in my life. Both were ten years older than me with different life styles, personalities and interests.

I met Elsie at a church meeting. I enjoyed her talk, saw her commitment and joy in what she was doing. Our friendship started slowly as I received wisdom and compassion from her. Elsie's love for alcoholics and their families opened my eyes to problems in my marriage. She took me to my first open A.A. meeting. The A.A. speaker was telling our story of the destruction alcohol created. His story of recovery gave me hope for my marriage.

℥ Mentors are able to go deeper into our lives.

℥ Sharing hard times opens the door for them to share their stories.

℥ They ask many questions and listen to our responses.

Elsie then took me to my first Al-Anon meeting where I met Rita. If I had not taken a risk to attend these meetings I would have missed having both women in my life for over fifty years. They mentored me through turbulent situations and opened up a new way to live regardless of the circumstances. It was tough going as I started to change. Six months later my husband found A.A. and sobriety until he died twenty-three years later.

"God provides the pieces of a puzzle. Look for them and be prepared to fit them into your life." Author Og Mandino

Rita

Five Words

Sometimes we can't find the proper words to express our sympathy or concern. Taking the time to encourage someone is not wasted. You may never know the impact of your words … go for it!

℈ You made a difference today.
℈ Come for lunch this week.
℈ Your call gave me hope.
℈ Call when you have time.
℈ Thanks for praying – I couldn't.

℈ You are precious to me.
℈ I'm always here for you.
℈ Your note gave me courage.
℈ Your questions made me think.

Words for Different People

NOTES TO A SPEAKER:

꒰ I'll remember your phrase ....

꒰ Your words encouraged me.

꒰ I loved the way you handled that situation.

꒰ You gave me many points to ponder.

꒰ I'm glad I didn't miss your presentation.

꒰ Thanks for sharing your life.

꒰ Your personal experiences gave me hope.

PASTORS, TEACHERS AND LEADERS:

꒰ Your sermon touched my life.

꒰ Thank you for explaining a difficult subject.

꒰ My attitude changed after I heard your personal struggles.

꒰ I'm so blessed to have you as my pastor, teacher, and leader.

꒰ You caused me to make a change in my life.

꒰ This course helped me make different choices.

꒰ Your message cleared up misconceptions.

Happiness Is

ℑ A day without interruptions.

ℑ Appreciating little moments.

ℑ Counting my blessings.

ℑ Laughing out loud.

ℑ Having friends over.

ℑ Taking a meal to someone.

ℑ Visiting old friends.

ℑ Making a treat for myself.

ℑ Looking at family pictures.

ℑ Watching favourite movies.

ℑ Volunteering your time.

ℑ Worshiping on Sunday.

ℑ Secretly doing something special for someone.

ℑ Making the call to connect with old friends.

Many years ago on a day when my life was too full, everything on my schedule was suddenly cancelled. I remember thinking, "I'm not going to fill it. I think I will just give myself this day and enjoy every moment!"

I still do this when the opportunity arises. Sometimes I read, take a nap, or walk through a florist shop and enjoy the beauty and smell the roses.

Chapter 4

"The only thing that counts is faith expressing itself through love." Galatians 5:6

Acts of Kindness

French poet Guillaume Apollinaire wrote: *"Now and then it is good to pause in our pursuit of happiness and just be happy."*

Recently I read that happiness is life's lubricant called laughter. Others tell stories of anonymously doing something helpful for another, and not getting found out. How wonderful is that.

Years ago we were challenged to "Do Acts of Kindness" every day. Getting ourselves out of the way opens up many areas to expand our energies and reap the rewards of helping someone without having to be recognized for it.

ॐ Write notes or letters to shut-ins, seniors or out of town friends.

ॐ Share what gives you a sense of comfort or serenity.

ॐ Invite someone over for coffee, lunch or dinner.

ॐ Write in a special journal remembering happy times.

ॐ Surprise someone anonymously.

ॐ Say encouraging words to someone.

ॐ Share your life.

Trusting and serving the Lord wherever He places you brings true happiness.

"Find a need and fill it." Dr. Robert H Schuller

Friendships

Friendship is a tapestry woven through the years with threads of joy, tears, love, laughter and happiness.

🙖 Friends bring out the best in you.
🙖 Friends do not need an invitation.
🙖 Friends see your need and show up.
🙖 Friends of many ages and life styles are precious.
🙖 Friends keep confidential information.
🙖 Friends challenge us.
🙖 Friends listen without condemnation.
🙖 Friends enlarge our world.
🙖 Friends can be relatives.

🙖 Friends can be work companions.
🙖 Friends can be neighbours.
🙖 Friends can be church members.
🙖 Friends can be opposite personalities.
🙖 Friends can be the same personalities.
🙖 Friends keep in touch.
🙖 Friends inspire and uplift you.
🙖 Friends share their life with you.
🙖 Friends are respectful.

"Actions, not words, are the true characteristic mark of the attachment of friends." George Washington

A New Friend

We purchased a home in 1971. A few days after our move my next door neighbour Lee came over to welcome our family into the neighbourhood. We had a common interest in music. Our four children were in a community band and it was noisy in our home. Lee was a pianist and often my husband, a singer, would try a new song at her home. Fourty-four years later we are still in touch.

I've been prompted to look into my different friendships and found the following points:

❧ One or two friends cannot fill all our needs or interests.

❧ Developing friendships takes time and effort.

❧ Shared values or belief systems allow us to go deeper.

❧ We can enjoy similar activities and interests together.

❧ Our time together often feels too short.

❧ Friends offer respect and caring.

꿈 Different ages bring new opportunities.

꿈 Sharing a hobby gives more time to talk.

꿈 Being spontaneous and available brings rewards.

꿈 Opposite life styles open our minds to different cultures, opinions and broadens our understanding.

꿈 The more you have in common the deeper your experiences can become.

꿈 Family commitments may change your available times.

꿈 Friendships come and go as lives change.

꿈 Getting older may shorten your times together.

꿈 Health issues can put limitations on outings.

Words To A Friend

ℑ Thanks for being my friend.

ℑ You made a difference in my life.

ℑ Your letter came after all the others stopped.

ℑ Thank you for your words of hope when I lost mine.

ℑ Your questions made me think.

ℑ I identified with your story.

ℑ Your time with me was special.

ℑ I like me when I'm with you.

ℑ Thanks for calling.

"Friendship is precious, not only in the shade but also in the sunshine of life." Thomas Jefferson

❧ Your call gave me hope.

❧ Thanks for stopping by.

❧ Thanks for listening to my problems.

❧ We never seem to have enough time.

❧ Thanks for praying when I couldn't.

"Nothing but heaven itself is better than a friend who is really a friend!" Plautus, Roman Playwright

Using Your Gifts

Everyone has been given gifts to use for others. Teaching, listening, serving and volunteering are a few. It's not about us. It's about helping others, who in turn use their gifts to encourage people who may only come into their lives for a short time. The following words may trigger a gift you never thought was yours.

HOSPITALITY comes in many forms.

ℑ Invite different people to your home.

ℑ Meet new friends for coffee or lunch.

HOBBIES can be shared or taught. Such as:

ℑ Knitting

ℑ Quilting

ℑ Photography

ℑ Making albums

ℑ Sewing

ℑ Board games such as Scrabble, Chess, Dominos

- Reading books to shut-ins.
- Start a book club that meets once a month.
- Sharing trips or leading a group on a trip.
- Driving people who don't drive or no longer are able to.

Talker and Listener

I was sent the following story about an elderly gentleman who was a widower. Mondays he was never available to go out, volunteer, drive or attend a dinner or function. His pastor was curious as to what this man did on Mondays and decided to pay him a visit.

"Well," the soft spoken man replied, *"After my wife died, my whole life seemed to be over. I prayed about it and asked the Lord to show me if there was anything left for me to do."*

He looked at his pastor and then continued, *"I seemed to have many areas that no longer were useful to anyone and it was very discouraging. Then I made a list of everything I loved doing. I knew I always was a talker and listener. I believe God was telling me to reach out to those who could no longer get out of their homes on their own. That is when I decided I would commit Mondays to calling whoever God put on my heart!"*

The pastor asked how many phone calls he usually made on a Monday.

"Well, it's usually at least twenty because I don't hurry the call and I listen for as long as the other person wants to talk."

This man had many gifts including compassion and encouragement. He no longer is lonely, in fact it seems he's busy and people look forward to his voice and enjoy their conversations with him.

What a wonderful world it would be if everyone took just one gift and used it to help, encourage or spend time with those who no longer are able leave their homes.

Perhaps one phone call would be enough to let them know they are not alone. Sometimes new friends are found just because one person gave them a call.

Art's 25th Anniversary Surprise

Planning surprises for unsuspecting people is a privilege. One year before our Bandmaster Art Smith's 25th year with the North Vancouver Youth Band, his health began declining. I was on the Board at the time and suggested we not wait to encourage him, but do it now. The Board agreed to host a surprise "This Is Your Life" celebration for him at the Vancouver Hotel based on the popular T.V. show at that time.

We began contacting friends, associates and past students without Art getting wind of the occasion. After many months completing snapshots of his life and inviting people who worked with him the big evening arrived.

Everyone kept the secret and were already seated at the hotel for a dinner. As the doors opened, an honour guard from his band led Art to the centre round table where his family awaited him. The room was filled with people; a special tiered cake plus guest speakers made it a memorable evening.

Looking at the pictures, I remember the look of surprise on Art's face. Memories of that evening will remain with me forever. The timing was perfect as Art was healthy and able to enjoy and experience the love and affection so many showed him. What an honour to recognize a unique individual who had given hours and years to bring music and encouragement to young people in our community.

Mom's 80th Birthday Surprise

Surprising my Mom on her 80th birthday was special. I don't think she ever had such a surprise. After retiring as a nanny, Mom was living in a seniors complex. My two daughters, Patti and Wendy booked the large reception room for the afternoon of her birthday.

I felt strongly this was the time to surprise her. The last couple of years she had recovered from a broken arm that had to be reset twice as well as having some balance issues.

One memory I always will have is the time she was not asked to cater a lunch for the complex. She always baked and made everything from sandwiches to desserts. Because of her broken arm the committee didn't ask her. Mom was very upset. I said, *"Mom you have a cast on your arm. The ladies knew you couldn't do it."*

Mom's reply was, *"I only have the cast on one arm. I still have my other!"*

The night before, Mom's sister from San Diego stayed with us and watched as we made special sandwiches and showed her the bible cake. My aunt said, *"This is the most fun I've ever had."*

Contacting the guests, writing the script for This Is Your Life along with putting all the pieces together in the room with balloons and food was a once in a lifetime event.

George and I were to take Mom for lunch on her birthday with another couple. She was so annoyed when I said I needed to borrow a special pan in the reception kitchen. She just wanted lunch.

When we opened the door everyone yelled, *"Surprise!"* Mom was shocked.

My husband read her story and one by one the special people behind the curtain came out.

46

Mom received so much love from old friends and was well enough to sit back and enjoy her day.

Some things can't wait. The following year Mom's cancer returned and she died in July. My family had the privilege to celebrate her and let her know how much she meant to us all.

When God nudges I hear the words, *"Just Do It."*

Surprise Kidnapped Weekend

Many years ago my friend Rita and I attended a Ladies Conference in California. Passing a ticket wicket on the grounds, we heard them announcing tickets were available for the Glory of Christmas event in December. Many times we often spoke of taking our husbands one year. Suddenly I said, *"Why don't we buy the tickets now and surprise them?"* We both said, *"Let's Do It!"* We paid for the tickets and immediately began planning how we could surprise Fred and George.

For the next six weeks we called each other, met to discuss how long we could keep it a secret and thoroughly enjoyed the magic of a surprise weekend in December. Our husbands began to think we were having trouble as the phone calls accelerated. Our plans progressed booking hotels, air flights, getting our clothes together and cancelling their engagements without them knowing it as the time got closer. We tried not to tell anyone, as we didn't want our secret to get out.

Finally the morning arrived and we four agreed to have breakfast near the airport across the border. Turned out the restaurant was closed and we had to have coffee in the bar.

Now two angry men just wanted to eat. Slowly, we both slipped a note across the table to them that read, *"Congratulations, our plane leaves in one hour for the Glory of Christmas in California."*

Our husbands looked shocked, questions were asked about appointments, suitcases and logistics. Rita and I laughed as we told them all the things we had to put together and what fun we had fooling them.

Boarding the plane, Fred said to the flight attendant, *"I've been kidnapped!"*

They never forgot the spontaneity of the surprise and the weekend was memorable!

Interruptions Can Look Like This

᠑ Sudden death of a loved one or close friend

᠑ Fatal accident

᠑ Unexpected job loss

᠑ Financial collapse

᠑ Spouse leaves

᠑ Divorce

᠑ Doctor's diagnosis

᠑ Death of a child

᠑ Friend abruptly leaves

᠑ Bankruptcy

᠑ Betrayal

᠑ Addictions

Interruptions can come with a knock on the door, a telephone call, an e-mail or cell phone text.

It can seem as if our life as we have known it disappears, leaving us in a place that has no easy answers. Disasters worldwide such as terrorist attacks, assassinations and others make us all remember exactly where we were during those times.

Chapter 5

"So don't be anxious about tomorrow. God will take care of your tomorrow too. Live one day at a time."
Matthew 6:34 (TLB)

Interruptions

Interruptions create unexpected changes in our lives disrupting what we thought was normal. We are unprepared and feel helpless to respond.

These times impact family, our friends and us, where we live and work as well as groups we belong to in our community. Sometimes what is left makes no sense.

How we accept, struggle through them and eventually deal with the immediate and after effects will challenge us in many areas. Interruptions test our faith and our perspective on life itself.

Reaching out to friends, family or professionals can calm our anxiousness when life is interrupted.

Alone – But Not Lonely

"You are precious in my eyes, and honoured, and I love you." Isaiah 43:4

After being married for forty-one years I became a widow. In one second, my life changed forever. Everything I knew seemed to be different. Here are a few examples:

ℑ Coming home to an empty apartment.

ℑ Eating out alone was difficult.

ℑ Setting my table for one.

ℑ Sleeping alone.

ℑ I seemed to notice only couples.

ℑ Quietness in my home.

ℑ No more cancer treatment appointments.

ℑ Memories made me weep.

All my decisions whether financial, personal, medical or social were challenging. It was time to be gentle, slow down and give myself permission to think and grieve.

Three months after my husband died I thought I was doing pretty well in my new life. I vividly remember attending a family dinner. It was time to say goodbye with hugs from everyone. I was the last to leave. Starting the engine, it suddenly hit me how alone I was and the tears began. I drove to the end of the street and stopped the car. I put my head on the steering wheel and cried for quite awhile. I felt like a giant earthquake had pulled everything out beneath me….but I survived and today I can say, *"Yes, I'm alone, but not lonely."*

"For I know the plans I have for you, declares the Lord, plans to prosper you and not to harm you, to give you hope and a future." Jeremiah 29:11

These are some of the steps I took to begin my journey alone recognizing life doesn't stay the same. I had choices and could be better or bitter.

ℨ I asked for God's guidance and went to church.

ℨ I allowed myself to get angry, grieve, and cry.

ℨ I wrote and dated my feelings in a journal.

ℨ I read my bible and marked special scriptures.

ℨ I contacted friends who also had been widowed.

ℨ I invited friends over for coffee.

When I thought I was losing my mind or just needed to talk things out I called other widows.

ℨ Sometimes I forgot which road to take off a highway.

ℨ When names of old friends disappeared I called my widow friends.

ℨ They would say, "It's just part of the process."

ℑ Sometimes, they'd say, "You're right on schedule."

ℑ "Don't worry, you're doing great, keep going."

ℑ They knew what I needed to hear.

ℑ I counted my blessings.

I attempted to write down three positive things. I couldn't do it every day, but when I did, I felt much better. Recently I found one of my early widow's journals. Reading my words it was like yesterday. Changes didn't happen quickly, but now I can encourage others as I listen to their stories.

Hints for Contentment

While visiting family members on Vancouver Island I happened to see a plaque in a small gift store that spelled out the subject of contentment.

> ❧ **Live Simply**
>
> ❧ **Love Generously**
>
> ❧ **Care Deeply**
>
> ❧ **Speak Kindly**

Aim to take the high road and **AVOID**:

❧ Complaining about anything, including the weather.

❧ Picturing yourself in any other circumstances or someplace else.

❧ Comparing your life with another.

❧ Allowing yourself to wish this or that had been otherwise.

❧ Dwelling on yesterday's problems.

❧ Fretting about tomorrow.

Chapter 6

"For I have learned to be content whatever the circumstances."
Philippians 4:11

Contentment

"There are only two ways to live your life. One is as though everything is a miracle or as though everything is a miracle." Albert Einstein

Every day is sprinkled with miracles waiting for you to enjoy. Expect to be surprised.

A friend gave me a little stand up plaque that I keep on my nightstand.

"You can't have a better tomorrow if you're thinking yesterday all the time."
Charles Francis Kettering

Give your troubles to God, he will be up all night anyway!

❦ Each life is like a book, lived one chapter at a time.

❦ Remember your wonderful moments.

"Never be in a hurry; do everything quietly and in a calm spirit. Do not lose your inner peace for anything whatsoever, even if your whole world seems upset." Saint Francis de Sales.

Helen Keller was born deaf, dumb and blind. She discovered a great secret. *"Life is an exciting business,"* she said. *"And it is most exciting when it is lived for others."*

These Are A Few of My Favourite Things

Memories are precious looking back at special places, celebrations, trips, and encounters alone or with other people. Visual items bring joy and blessings as we remember those times.

When I moved, my oldest son Don said, *"Mom we'll take your sewing machine to the dump."* Horrified, I said, *"No, I'm not ready to give it up."* I have so many wonderful memories of Mom sewing my clothes. She taught me to sew and made dresses for me including for my wedding party and my wedding gown.

Carrying on that heritage, I made dresses for Christmas and Easter for my two daughters. I found myself sewing bridesmaid dresses for them. Many last minute requests came from friends and neighbours, as many had never learned to sew.

A few weeks after putting my sewing machine in my storage room I flipped over a magazine page and found a picture of a remodelled Singer sewing machine with a tabletop. Suddenly, I  had a project. I called my friend Wilma and shared about finding the picture.

She said, *"Leta, maybe my husband Woody, could put a top on it for you."*

I was so excited and asked Dennis, my youngest son if he could take it all apart except the sides, treadle and the Singer word holding it together.

He came over the next week and while taking the machine apart said, *"Mom, there's something stuck in here."*

He pulled out a small piece of cardboard that read "Seam Binding 3 yards 19 cents."

More of My Favourite Things

Many years ago my youngest daughter and I decided to browse an antique store. We both ended up purchasing a surprise for Christmas. Neither of us knew the other had bought what we both had admired. Every time I place my earrings on that special plate, I smile and remember our day together.

I found a wonderful poem by Bonnie Mohr called, *"Living Life"* that gives me a warm and special feeling every time I read it hanging in my hallway.

- The cover for this book is an oil painting from my friend Cindy that I treasure.

- Pictures on my walls are memories of different times.

- Various items I've bought on trips.

- Special gifts I've received from friends and family.

- My bible has dates, names and notes in it.

- A special box holds letters, cards and poems from family members and others. On a rainy day, I pull these treasures out and find enjoyment over and over again.

ℑ I love to change things around in my home as it creates a different look. Often visitors are interested, notice an item and ask for the story.

ℑ I had a surprise 65th birthday party and treasure the binder with comments from the guests.

ℑ Family albums with pictures and comments are memory reminders of earlier times.

ℑ Books have always been important for me.

Items are lost treasures if they are always tucked away in drawers. You cannot enjoy your favourite memories if you do not have the opportunity to see and remember those special times.

Unexpected Phone Call

A phone call brought an unexpected friend into my life. I had seen her in church on Sundays but we had never spent time together. Listening to her I realized our husbands shared a common addiction with alcohol. My husband had found sobriety in A.A. but her husband was struggling and was the reason for her call.

Over coffee at her house, I suggested she try Al-Anon, which had helped me. The following weeks we went to Al-Anon meetings and continued to share our lives. Not long after her husband accepted a new job in another province and they moved.

Although I've lost touch with her, I continue to pray our times together helped as I sip my morning coffee in the special mug she gave me.

There are no coincidences. We may never know how a single phone call can encourage us. It takes two to make it work. One to call … another to answer. It was that way for me many years ago.

What Gives Me Joy

℣ Time with family and friends.

℣ Inviting a friend for coffee.

℣ Giving a gift to lift someone's spirit.

℣ Preparing lunch or dinner for a friend, neighbour or ill person.

℣ Leading a woman's study group.

℣ Listening to a sermon that inspires me to action.

℣ My quiet time with God early in the morning.

℣ Giving away something I have to someone who needs it.

℣ Organizing a surprise for someone.

℣ Signing up for something I've always wanted to do.

℣ Knitting for a friend, new baby or family member.

꽃 Early morning walks on the seawall.

꽃 Sitting outside on my balcony with a good book.

꽃 Catching up in person with a friend.

꽃 Finding a gift that someone needed.

꽃 Watching a favourite movie with no interruptions.

꽃 Taking a friend or family member to a football game.

꽃 Completing family albums with pictures and quotes.

꽃 Sending cards and newspaper clippings to those I know would enjoy them.

꽃 Planning and going with a friend on a trip.

Time

Many years ago at a Ladies Conference in Garden Grove, California, I heard author and international public speaker Zig Ziglar. He never accepts a speaking engagement if he cannot be home in time to teach his Sunday School class.

His personal story touched my heart. One evening after dinner he and his son were playing Monopoly for a long time. They both had cash in the bank, hotels, railroads, etc. when suddenly his wife appeared and said, *"Time for bed."* Everything they had collected had to be put away in the box.

Zig said, *"Without warning our game was over."* All the time and effort he and his son had given to Monopoly had ended.

As humans, we too one day will hear a call. It may come early in life or much later. Our busy lives filled with work, families, friends, community, church, sports, hobbies and fun will cease. It will all go into a box...except what we have stored up for eternity.

Our time is a commodity we all have. Our time is ours to keep for ourselves or we can choose to share it with others.

"Do not store up for yourselves treasures on earth, where moth and rust destroy, and where thieves break in and steal. But store up for yourselves treasures in heaven, where moth and rust do not destroy, and where thieves do not break in and steal. For where your treasure is, there your heart will be also."

Matthew 6:19-21

Time, A Precious Gift

"There is a time for everything, and a season for every activity under heaven." Ecclesiastes 3:1

ᔓ Few things in life are given to us in equal amounts.

ᔓ Every person has twenty-four hours of time each day.

ᔓ We are free to choose how we spend it.

ᔓ Friends move away and we lose touch.

ᔓ Jobs that once offered security disappear.

ᔓ Health issues slow us down.

ॐ Growing up it seems that time moves very quickly.

ॐ Suddenly the teen age years arrive and the clock moves faster.

ॐ Before we know it we are married.

ॐ Perhaps children follow in the next years.

ॐ One day we will find ourselves in the winter season of our life.

ॐ Projects we always were going to pursue we cannot do anymore.

ॐ Health issues or family concerns take our focus.

Sometimes the death of a loved one gives us no time to say goodbye.

Every Day Count Your Blessings

❧ Smile

❧ Laugh

❧ Call a friend

❧ Walk outside

❧ Be enthusiastic

❧ Help someone

❧ Look for beauty in people

❧ Read uplifting books

❧ Make good choices

❧ Play music

❧ Relax

❧ Listen to someone

❧ Stop talking

❧ Breathe deeply

❧ Eat healthy

❧ Clear clutter

❧ Be enthusiastic

❧ Think before answering

Chapter 7

"Teach us to number our days and recognize how few they are; help us to spend them as we should." Psalm 90:12 (TLB)

Gift of Morning

Every morning as I spend time with God I come away with renewed hope, faith and encouragement. I love the quietness with no interruptions to read my devotional books before my day begins. A friend said he lights a candle and I light a tea light.

Jesus took time to go to His heavenly Father to pray and listen. He went away by himself even when pressures and His disciples wanted Him to continue healing, preaching and giving comfort.

Looking back, I see God's leading in my life. Sometimes I have no immediate answers. Other times it is very clear as the scriptures for that day are exactly what I needed to read and put into my day. If I don't make this a priority, I get side tracked and my morning is gone.

Writing in my journal daily helps me see His leading when I seem to be totally exasperated, angry or impatient waiting for His direction. Mornings have brought me closer to Him.

Answers to prayers come in His time with a yes, no or wait. His schedule has always been the right one.

"Each day is a day that God has given us, and each moment of that day is in His hands." Roy Lessin

Live In The Moment

See each day as an opportunity for something new and wonderful to happen.

ᔑ Set your days up with some wiggle room for the unexpected.

ᔑ Being flexible allows for surprises that have to be answered immediately.

Could you use two tickets to a wonderful concert tonight?

ᔑ I have to go out of town tonight, can you use my two hockey tickets for tomorrow?

ᔑ I was just given two free dinners this weekend, can you pick them up?

70

Often I have been given many free passes to events because I have been flexible and able to make arrangements to pick up the free tickets.

One morning during a busy Christmas week in early December I got a call from a special friend. She had won a free weekend for two to San Francisco that had to be used within four days.

My two daughters and I had a ladies retail store and December is very hectic. Both of them said, *"Go for it Mom, we can handle the store."* My friend Rita and I had a marvellous time.

What opportunities could be out there if we took **BUSY** out of our life?

White Spaces

Life is too short to fill every minute with things to accomplish or do. Leaving white or empty spaces in our lives are choices we make ahead of time. I've never regretted being available…but being too busy has been costly.

Blessings come in various forms including unexpected invitations as well as:

⌇ Opportunities to renew old friendships or acquaintances.

⌇ A call may offer a once in a lifetime experience.

⌇ An uninterrupted time to enjoy someone.

⌇ A new friend may be introduced to you.

A special morning happened when my cousin Kathy flew into our city. Years ago she stayed with us for a few days. She had a couple of hours before her cruise ship departed. We keep in touch but distance has never given us the opportunity to meet one on one. Her delay at the airport gave us time to share a breakfast, many cups of coffee and uninterrupted time to catch up with our lives and families.

Kathy and I at the airport.

Changing your schedule may bring a blessing you never expected.

Choices

We make choices regarding our life path, our desires and how we deal with difficult situations. Choices about:

℩ Schooling

  ℩ Courses

    ℩ Dating

      ℩ Marriage Partners

    ℩ Friends

      ℩ Hobbies

Fanny Crosby, blinded at age six wrote over 9,000 poems. She decided to be content and make the most of every circumstance. She died at age 95.

℩ What we put into our mind shapes our values and beliefs.

  ℩ It also affects our view of the world and ourselves.

    ℩ Choices influence how we use our time.

      ℩ Our choices form our character.

        ℩ Our choices determine where we live.

The Choices We Make

Life is like a beautiful buffet table filled with color, food, flowers and candles. Different tantalizing dishes are beautifully arranged to appeal to our senses. All will be wasted unless we pick up a plate and begin to fill it. Sometimes we have to try a new food before we can decide if we really like it or not.

Asking questions is an excellent way to make better choices.

At my yearly check up with my doctor I asked him, *"Why is it so hard to lose weight especially around the middle as I get older?"*

He stopped what he was writing, put down his pen and looked directly at me. *"Mrs. Jones,"* he said, *"it's whatever you put into your mouth!"*

Whenever I have a choice to make regarding foods I purchase or eat, his encouraging words have helped me make healthier decisions.

"Start by doing what's necessary, then do what's possible and suddenly you're doing the impossible." St. Francis of Assissi.

Encouraging Others

Consider Writing Notes to the following people:

- ℑ Graduation students
- ℑ New neighbours
- ℑ New mothers
- ℑ Those who finally landed a job
- ℑ Those who passed a difficult exam
- ℑ A new pastor, teacher or principal
- ℑ A relative or friend

Reckless words pierce like a sword, but the tongue of the wise brings healing." Proverbs 12:1

Notes and Cards Are Appreciated By:

❦ Those recovering in hospital

❦ Those separated or divorced

❦ Patients recuperating at home

❦ Grieving the death of a loved one

❦ After a misunderstanding with a friend

"Keep interested in others and keep interested in the wide and wonderful world." Frederic March

Voicemail

Voicemail messages from a loving friend can be uplifting. Sometimes, just the sound of another person's voice can break our darkness and may give us strength to go on. Those who live alone, or have no support system or family members nearby especially need to hear a live voice if they are:

❦ Going through a difficult time

❦ Experiencing separation, divorce or a death

❦ Being transferred or have had a job loss

❦ Facing health issues

❦ Depressed or anxious

People who live alone could feel someone cares if messages like the following are heard:

- ೫ I'm thinking about you.
- ೫ I'd like to give you a hug.
- ೫ I love you.
- ೫ Please know that you're missed.
- ೫ Tomorrow will be better.
- ೫ Can I bring you a coffee?
- ೫ Are you up for a visit?

Special Reminders

Taking the time to send a basket, wrapped gift or flowers if you know your friend is hurting is never a bad idea..but it has to be pursued and completed.

One special memory I have is the time I came home after visiting my husband in his last days in the hospital. Weary and mentally tired, I found at my door a basket filled with everything I needed for a healthy meal. I was too tired to even think of fixing something to eat. Included with the meal were napkins, chocolates, a bottle of water, homemade cookies and a wee note that read, "Take care of yourself and eat tonight."

Fixing an interesting basket can be as simple as a package of Caesar salad along with a chicken pie, quiche, or a one plate meal to heat, homemade squares, fruit or drinks. It takes minutes to put it together with an encouraging note…try it and you'll make someone feel special.

All of our thoughts to do something mean nothing unless it happens. If you know someone is struggling, do something to give hope and let that person know she is loved and is not alone.

I heard of a beautifully wrapped box that was filled with personal items including, fragrant soap, bubble bath, a small tube of hand cream, body lotion, lip gloss, shampoo and all of them were wrapped in a soft pastel tissue. Anyone needing a touch of kindness would appreciate this gift.

Memory Moments

JOURNAL WRITING:

꿈 Journaling helps us remember what can we easily forget

꿈 Life is full of memory moments

꿈 Date and list happy times

꿈 First dates, births, graduations, house purchases

SPECIAL EVENTS:

꿈 Honeymoon memories

꿈 Plane or boat trips

꿈 Celebrations such as reunions

Journaling times of difficult feelings due to interruptions in our lives are a way of seeing how we've changed over the years. It's also an important tool in understanding ourselves and what was happening then in our families and our world.

Finding only one card with my Mom's writing was special. A letter written by my husband before we were married gave me a look at what he was thinking back then in his own hand writing.

Chapter 8

"Be still before the Lord and wait patiently for Him."
Psalm 37:7

Under Construction

Have you ever considered how God, our architect, continues to refine, define and change us?

I'm under construction again!

September 13, 1993 changed my life when I became a widow. Four months later I moved. Only God could have orchestrated how I found the two storey corner apartment with an unobstructed majestic view of the Lions Mountains. Going from a basement to sunlight I've experienced blossoming trees, hummingbirds on my hanging baskets and witnessed the changing seasons.

Eighteen years later after a relaxing, quiet day sorting and throwing out files the unpredictable happened. I had been working for four or five hours when I stood up to go to another room.

Immediately, I felt as if I was on a turbulent sea aboard a ship. Swaying from side to side, I held onto the walls until I managed to get back to my chair.

"Call the Nurse's Line," I told myself, something is definitely wrong. The nurse after hearing my story asked numerous questions. My answers were no, just my balance is off. I told her I hadn't eaten since noon and maybe if I had some soup it would help.

I remember clearly her next sentence. *"If anything different occurs, immediately go to the hospital."* She repeated this three times.

Hanging onto my kitchen counter I managed to eat the soup and continued to sit for half an hour. Suddenly, an acidic taste came into my mouth. This was different. The nurse's warning rang in my ears. My daughter drove me to the emergency ward where I was hospitalized for three days before being released. Tests determined I had suffered a mini stroke.

Arriving home, I saw new construction across the street was a block long. I felt under construction in a different way. It began with my follow-up doctor's appointment.

I was not to go anywhere by myself, no driving for at least three to six months, relax, take it easy and listen to your body my doctor told me.

Being independent all my life, I struggled with the changes. Learning to let go was not easy. In fact, it was downright painful. Asking for rides to the doctor's office or shopping was proving hard for me. I displayed pride and other unbecoming character defects. These were lessons God was showing me. Habits are difficult to change. Blessings were coming.

My morning devotional time was extended, as I didn't have to be anywhere. Driving friends, leading a woman's study and mentoring were a few commitments I had to release. I was in recovery. One morning as I prayed I realized I might never drive again. I read an encouraging scripture, *"So don't be anxious about tomorrow. God will take care of your tomorrow too. Live one day at a time."* Matthew 6:34 (TLB)

Twenty-seven stairs down to do my laundry would have to wait as I reached out for help. This was a new experience. More questions surfaced. Would I have to move? Where to? I opened my bible and read Psalm 46:10 *"Be still and know that I am God."* I felt His assurance and peace.

One afternoon my daughter Patti popped in and said, *"Mom, I want to ask you a few questions about the new blood pressure medication."* After answering them, she said, *"I think the new medication is the problem. You have all the possible side effects."* I immediately booked a doctor's appointment and told him what we thought and he agreed that I needed to go back onto my old costly blood pressure pill.

Within a week, my balance was back. My doctor said, *"I don't think you had a stroke as you responded so quickly. It was likely the new blood pressure medication."*

Prayers were answered! I am driving again, writing and taking more time to enjoy life. A friend recently remarked how sad that I will lose the magnificent view I have from my balcony.

My response was, *"I have enjoyed the view and the Lions Mountains for eighteen years. How special is that?"*

Sometimes a wake-up call like a health set back, forces us to look at our lives differently. Each day is a gift not to be wasted. My life is in God's hands and He can see around the corner when I cannot.

"Never live in the past, but always learn."
2008 Friendship Book

God's Blueprint For Your Life

Many years ago I learned to drive on a stick shift car. An old friend offered to teach me. He was very patient as I had many stops, starts, stalls and jerky movements. Over time I found the balance between using the gas pedal and easing the clutch into the right position to go forward smoothly.

It didn't happen quickly. In the following weeks, my instructor guided me over many different roads and parking spaces in all kinds of weather, hot, cold and wet.

In order to have a driver's license I had to read the Manual, practice with a friend, show up at the Motor Vehicle Branch and drive with an unknown inspector. Passing or failing depend on his recommendation.

Where do we learn how to have a fulfilling life in spite of our unrealistic expectations? I believe our manual, blueprint or map is the Bible. Inside this book are stories of real people.

One of my favourite books is Proverbs. You can't misunderstand the message.

"Without wood a fire goes out; without gossip a quarrel dies down." Proverbs 26:20

God has a plan for everyone. How comforting to know that the Architect who made everything, including us, gave the Bible in order for us to have a blueprint to follow.

Unexpected Gestures

As an only child, brought up by my single Mom, with all family relatives living in another province, I looked forward to having in-laws one day. It took many years before I had a good relationship with my mother-in-law. One special day she said to her son, *"I don't want you to take me shopping, I want to go with Leta as she never hurries me!"* I never expected to hear those words, but it encouraged me.

Some years ago one of my son-in-laws, James, presented me with thirteen red roses on Valentine's Day. I asked him how come and he replied, *"Because I wanted to!"*

It caught me by surprise and was such a beautiful gesture. Usually it's the wives who get the flowers on this day. I think maybe it was the first year after my husband died.

One of my daughter-in-laws, Sally, inserted the following poem into my birthday card in the 1990's. I have kept it and was encouraged by it.

TO HIS MOTHER
"Mother-in-law" they say,
   and yet,
Somehow I simply can't
   forget
'Twas you who watched his baby ways,
Who taught him his first hymn of praise,
Who smiled on him with loving pride,
When he first toddled by your side.
"Mother-in-law" but oh, 'twas you
Who taught him to be kind and true;
When he was tired, almost asleep,
'Twas to your arms he used to creep.
And when he bruised his tiny knee,
'Twas you who kissed it tenderly.
"Mother-in-law" they say, and yet,
Somehow I never shall forget
How much I owe
To you, who taught him how to grow.
You trained your son to look above,
You made of him the man I love.
And so I think of that today
When with thankful heart I'll say,
"Our mother."
                         — ANONYMOUS

Many years ago I attended a convention in Victoria. The speaker closed her presentation with a poem titled "The Cross In My Pocket" by Mrs. Verna May Thomas. It has always been an encouragement to me.

The Cross In My Pocket

The poem goes … I carry a cross in my pocket, a simple reminder to me of the fact that I am a Christian no matter where I may be.

This little cross is not magic, nor is it a good luck charm. It isn't meant to protect me from every physical harm.

It's not for identification for the entire world to see. It's simply an understanding between my Saviour and me.

When I put my hand in my pocket to bring out a coin or a key, the cross is there to remind me of the price He paid for me.

It reminds me too, to be thankful for my blessings day by day, and to strive to serve Him better in all that I do and say.

It's also a daily reminder of the peace and comfort I share with all who know my Master and give themselves to His care.

So, I carry a cross in my pocket reminding no one but me that Jesus Christ is Lord of my life if only I'll let Him be.

Encouraging Books

If you don't read good books, you'll read bad books."
C. S. Lewis

I grew to love books as a young child during a time I was bed ridden. I've never lost the excitement of spending hours with a good book. My husband used to say when he saw me reading, *"I've lost you again."*

A few of my favourite books are listed below with comments and insights.

Beauty Care For The Tongue by LeRoy Koopman

An excellent book with a study guide. All about words and their impact. A physician told me that the tongue has the most muscles of any organ in our body.

In His Steps by Charles M. Sheldon

I read this once a year. Stories of a group of people who made a commitment to "not make a decision without asking themselves, *What would Jesus do?*" This book has sold millions of copies and Charles life story is very interesting on how he lost the copyright.

The Purpose Driven Life by Rick Warren

In 1970 I prayed a specific prayer for people in churches. Eventually, I stopped praying and forgot about it. I was given this book for Christmas 2003. My heart almost stopped when I recognized my prayer many years before had been answered as Celebrate Recovery had just started in California. God never forgets our prayers. *A book for individuals or a group study.* Finding your purpose in life is exciting.

Norman Rockwell's America by Reader's Digest

I grew up seeing his wonderful illustrations on the covers of The Saturday Evening Post magazine. He captured many historical events as well as everyday pictures. Norman's life story, setbacks and how he handled the hurdles continue to give me hours of enjoyment whenever I pick up this book…including many chuckles.

Sometimes a single line, picture or story helped or inspired me.

Uplifting Scriptures

Here is a list of scriptures that I go to which is, written by Father Heart Communication, 1999, titled, *"Father's Love Letter.com."*

My Child ... God Really Loves You

You may not know Me, but I know everything about you.
Psalm 139:1

I know when you sit down, and when you rise up, I am familiar with all your ways.
Psalm 139:2-3

For you were made in My image.
Genesis 1:27

Even the very hairs on your head are numbered.
Matthew 10:29-31

For you were made in My image. Genesis 1:27

In Me you live and move and have your being for you are My offspring. Acts 17:28

I knew you even before you were conceived. Jeremiah 1:4-50

I chose you when I planned creation. Ephesians 1-11-12

You were not a mistake, for all your days are written in My book. Psalm 139:15-16

I determined the exact time of your birth and where you would live. Acts 17:26

You are fearfully and wonderfully made, I knit you together in your mother's womb. Psalm 13-14

And brought you forth on the day you were born. Psalm 71:6

I have been misrepresented by those who don't know Me. John 8:41-44

I am not distant and angry, but am the complete expression of love. 1 John 4:16

And it is My desire to lavish my love on you. John 3:1

Simply because you are my child and I am your Father. 1John 3:1

I offer you more than your earthly father ever could. Matthew 7:11

For I am the perfect Father. Matthew 5:48

Every good gift that you receive comes from My hand. James 1:17

For I am your provider and I meet all your needs. Matthew 6:31-33

My plan for your future has always been filled with hope. Jeremiah 29:11

Because I love you with an everlasting love. Jeremiah 31:3

My thoughts toward you are countless as the sand on the seashore. Psalm 139:17-18

And I rejoice over you with singing. Zephaniah 3:17

I will never stop doing good to you. Jeremiah 32:40

For you are my treasured possession. Exodus 19:5

I desire to establish you with all My heart and all My soul. Jeremiah 33:3

And I want to show you great and marvellous things. Jeremiah 33:3

If you seek Me with all your heart, you will find Me. Deuteronomy 4:29

Delight in Me and I will give you the desires of your heart. Psalm 37:4

For it is I who gave you those desires. Philippians 2:13

I am able to do more for you than you could possibly imagine. Ephesians 3:20

When you are broken-hearted, I am close to you. Psalm 34:18

As a shepherd carries a lamb, I have carried you close to my heart. Isaiah 40:11

And I'll take away all the pain you have suffered on this earth.
Revelation 21:3-4

I am your Father and I love you even as I love my Son, Jesus.
John 17:23

For in Jesus, My love for you is revealed. John:26

He is the exact representation of My being. Hebrews 1:3

He came to demonstrate that I am for you, not against you.
Romans 8:31

And to tell you that I am not counting your sins.
2 Corinthians 5:18-19

I am also the Father who comforts you in all your troubles.
2 Corinthians 1:3-4

His death was the ultimate expression of My love for you.
1 John 4:10

I gave up everything I loved that I might gain your love.
Romans 8:31-32

If you receive the gift of my Son Jesus, you receive Me.
1 John 2:23

And nothing will ever separate you from My love again.
Romans 8:38-39

Come home and I'll throw the biggest party heaven has ever seen.

Luke 15:7

I have always been Father, and will always be Father.

Ephesians 3:14-15

For I am your greatest Encourager.

2 Thessalonians 2:16-17

Will You Be My Child.

John 1:12-13

I am waiting for you.

Luke 15:11-32

Love, Your Dad — Almighty God

Final Thoughts

Thank you for reading my book. I hope it will give you more ways to encourage others and yourself! My prayer is that you will know God is always with you.

May you feel His presence in your life and know He loves you dearly.

By: Leta Jones

Made in the USA
Charleston, SC
13 December 2015